Dear Parent:
Your child's love of reading starts here!

Every child learns to read in a different way and at his or her own speed. Some go back and forth between reading levels and read favorite books again and again. Others read through each level in order. You can help your young reader improve and become more confident by encouraging his or her own interests and abilities. From books your child reads with you to the first books he or she reads alone, there are I Can Read Books for every stage of reading:

SHARED READING
Basic language, word repetition, and whimsical illustrations, ideal for sharing with your emergent reader

BEGINNING READING
Short sentences, familiar words, and simple concepts for children eager to read on their own

READING WITH HELP
Engaging stories, longer sentences, and language play for developing readers

READING ALONE
Complex plots, challenging vocabulary, and high-interest topics for the independent reader

I Can Read Books have introduced children to the joy of reading since 1957. Featuring award-winning authors and illustrators and a fabulous cast of beloved characters, I Can Read Books set the standard for beginning readers.

A lifetime of discovery begins with the magical words **"I Can Read!"**

Visit www.icanread.com for information
on enriching your child's reading experience.

Visit www.zonderkidz.com for more Zonderkidz I Can Read! titles.

A Savior has been born to you.
He is Christ the Lord.
—Luke 2:11

ZONDERKIDZ

Jesus, God's Great Gift
Copyright © 2010 by Zondervan
Illustrations © 2010 by Dennis G. Jones

An **I Can Read Book**

Requests for information should be addressed to:
Zondervan, 3900 *Sparks Drive SE, Grand Rapids, Michigan 49546*

Ebook ISBN 978-0-310-42456-7

Library of Congress Cataloging-in-Publication Data
Jesus, God's Great Gift / pictures by Dennis G. Jones.
   p. cm.
   ISBN 978-0-310-71881-9 (softcover)
   1. Jesus Christ—Nativity—Juvenile literature. 2. Christmas—Juvenile literature. I. Jones,
     Dennis G., 1956-
   BT315.3.J48 2010
   232.92—dc22   2009022675

All Scripture quotations, unless otherwise indicated, are taken from the Holy Bible,
New International Version®, NIV®. Copyright © 1973, 1978, 1984 by Biblica, Inc.® Used by
permission of Zondervan. All rights reserved worldwide.

Any internet addresses (websites, blogs, etc.) and telephone numbers printed in this book
are offered as a resource. They are not intended in any way to be or imply an endorsement
by Zondervan, nor does Zondervan vouch for the content of these sites and numbers for the
life of this book.

No part of this publication may be reproduced, stored in a retrieval system, or transmitted
in any form or by any means—electronic, mechanical, photocopy, recording, or any
other—except for brief quotations in printed reviews, without the prior permission of the
publisher.

Published in association with the literary agency of Alive Communications, Inc.,
8585 Criterion Drive Unit 63060, Colorado Springs, CO 80920-1045.
www.alivecommunications.com

Zonderkidz is a trademark of Zondervan.

I Can Read® and I Can Read Book® are trademarks of HarperCollins Publishers.

Editor: Mary Hassinger
Art direction and design: Sarah Molegraaf

Printed in China

21 22 23 24 /DSC/ 24 23 22 21 20 19 18 17 16 15 14 13 12 11 10 9

JESUS
God's Great Gift

pictures by Dennis G. Jones

An important man told people to go to their hometowns. Mary and Joseph had to go to Bethlehem. It was a very long walk.

Mary was going to have a baby soon.

She was so tired.

The donkey was tired too.

Joseph decided to find a place

for them to sleep.

Joseph knocked on the first door.

A man answered.

"I have no room for you!"

the man said.

Joseph knocked on another door.

A woman answered.

"I have no room for you!"
the woman said.

Joseph kept walking.

He knocked on another door.

A bald man answered.

"I have no room for you!"
the man said.

Joseph kept walking.

He knocked on another door.

An old man answered.

His inn was full too.

Bethlehem was so busy.

Every place Joseph went was full.

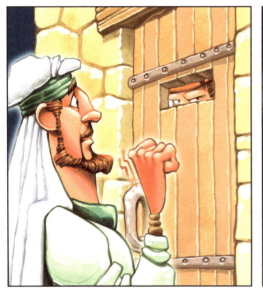

Joseph walked to the last house.

He knocked on the door.

A man answered.

This man had no room,

but he wanted to help Joseph.

He had a place

for Mary and Joseph to sleep.

He told Joseph to follow him.

That place was the barn!

Mary and Joseph were happy.

The donkey was happy.

Joseph and Mary were tired.

They decided to sleep in the barn.

Mary sat down.

She said to Joseph,

"I'm going to have the baby."

Soon, baby Jesus was born.

A big star went over the barn

to show that Jesus was God's son.

Mary held her new baby.

She knew Jesus was special.

While Mary was taking care of Jesus, shepherds were taking care of sheep. They did not see the big star that was over the barn.

The shepherds sat around a big fire.

Then, something started to happen.

Bright lights came.

The shepherds didn't see the lights.

The lights were angels!

The angels scared the shepherds.

The angels sang about Jesus and praised God.

One angel told the shepherds,

"Jesus was born in Bethlehem."

"He will save the world," the angel said.

"He's in a manger. Go see him."

The angel pointed to the barn.

The shepherds ran to the barn.

Mary took Jesus out of the manger.

She held him in her lap.

The shepherds praised Jesus.

Later, they told everyone.

Jesus grew up.

Mary and Joseph moved

to a real house.

The star from over the barn

was over the new house now.

Wise men had been following the star for a long time. They knew the star meant a special baby had been born.

The wise men came to the house.

One of the men knocked on the door.

Mary and Joseph answered.

They didn't know the wise men.

They didn't know why

the wise men had come.

The wise men bowed down.

They praised Jesus.

They gave Jesus gifts

that showed how important he was.

When Jesus grew up,

he started to do special things.

He told people about God,

and he saved us from our sins.